THE OBSCURE WORLD OF DIEDRE AND ALBERT

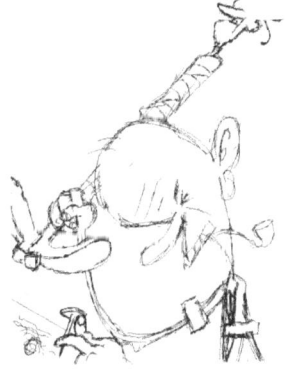

ANDREW JOHNSON

THE OBSCURE WORLD OF DIEDRE AND ALBERT

WRITTEN BY ANDREW JOHNSON AND ALEX
WYNDHAM BAKER

DRAWN BY ANDREW JOHNSON

DEDICATION

THIS BOOK IS DEDICATED TO THOSE
PEOPLE THAT MOSTLY DON'T TEND
TO THINK IN STRAIGHT LINES

ACKNOWLEDGMENTS

THANK YOU TO MY LOVELY WIFE FOR NOT KICKING
MY HEAD IN WHILE I AM DOING THIS SORT OF THING
AND TO MY BEAUTIFUL CHILDREN FOR KICKING MY
HEAD IN, BUT ONLY AT THE CORRECT MOMENTS
WHEN I NEED IT THE MOST...

BIG THANKS TO ALEX WYNDHAM BAKER IN HELPING
CORRECT
SOME ERRANT GRAMMAR AND FOR HIS ALL ROUND
CLEVER AND INSPIRATIONAL WORDYNESS

I WOULD ALSO LIKE TO ACKNOWLEDGE THAT
WITHOUT HAVING CONVERSATIONS WITH CERTAIN
PEOPLE AS TO THE TRUTH OF WHAT MARROW FAT
PEAS ACTUALLY ARE,
THEIR ORIGIN AND WHY THEY ARE CALLED MARROW
FAT PEAS,
THAT NONE OF THIS WOULD BE POSSIBLE OR MAKE
ANY SENSE. WHICH, OF COURSE, IT DOESN'T.

BUT THAT IS ENOUGH ABOUT YOOTHA JOYCE

THE OBSCURE WORLD OF DIEDRE AND ALBERT

DIEDRE AND ALBERT ARE A RETIRED COUPLE WHO LIVE ALMOST VERY HAPPILY IN A MINISCULE FOOD BLENDER ON THE EDGE OF SOME FAR OFF PSYCHOTIC UNIVERSE.

THEY LIKE TO PASS THE TIME COOKING, WATCHING TV, KEEPING THE HOUSE TIDY, EMPLOYING CASUAL VIOLENCE AND EATING PEOPLE.

CONTENT

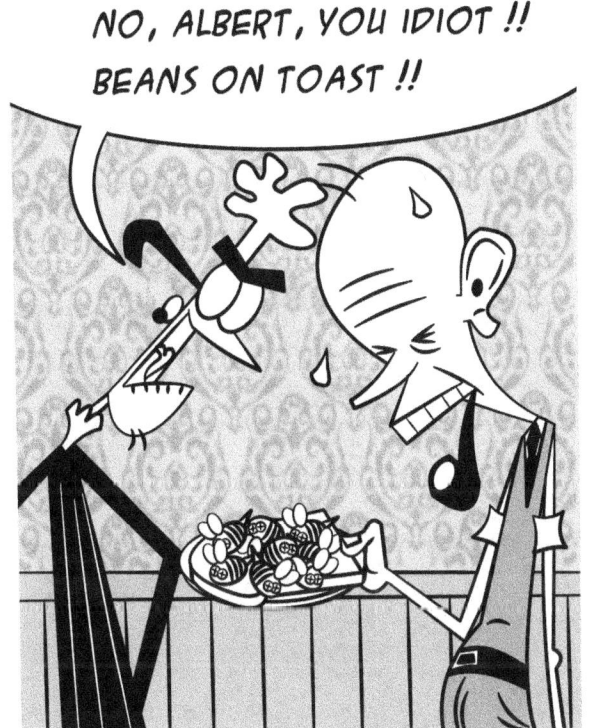

ALBERT WOULD OFTEN COOK BREAKFAST WITH A KEEN EYE AND A DEAF EAR FOR MODERN CUISINE.

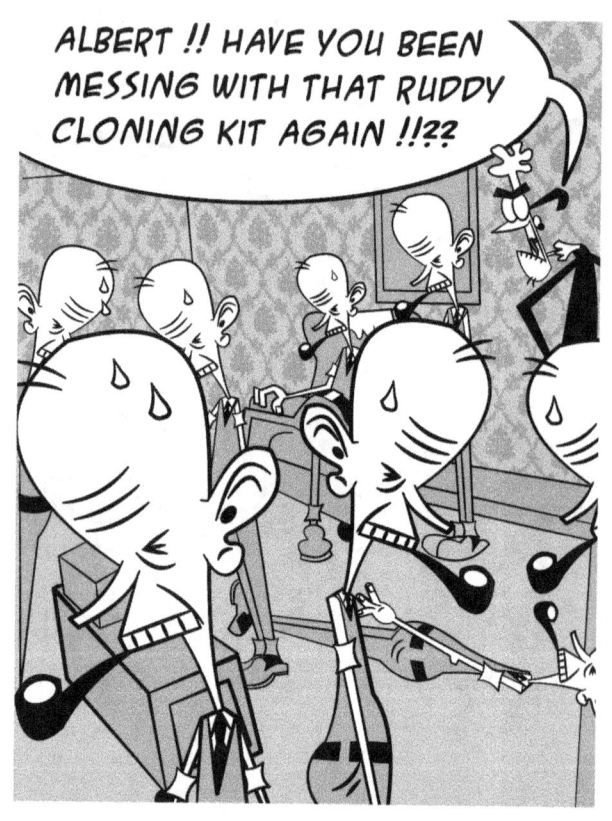

BOREDOM FREQUENTLY LED ALBERT
DOWN NEW RECREATIONAL AVENUES.

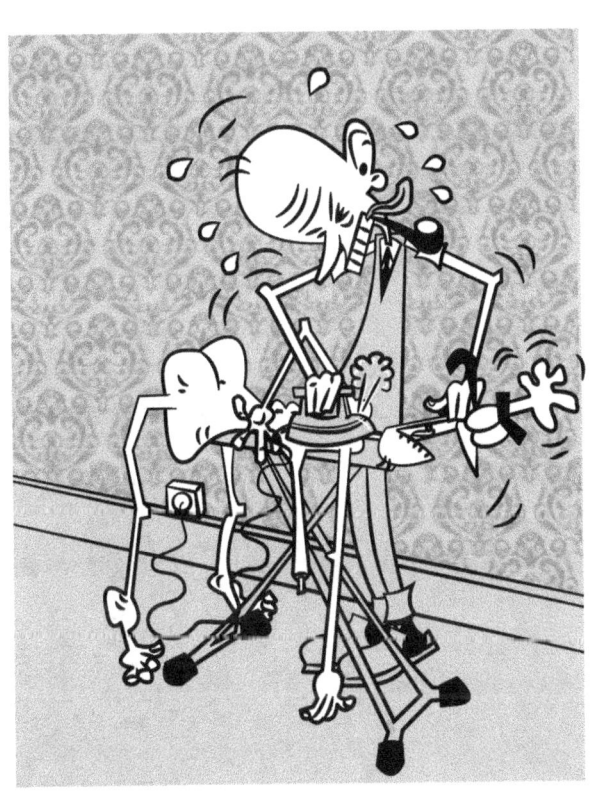

ALBERTS SKILL WITH A HOT
IRON WAS SOMETHING DIEDRE
FOUND TO BE VERY USEFUL

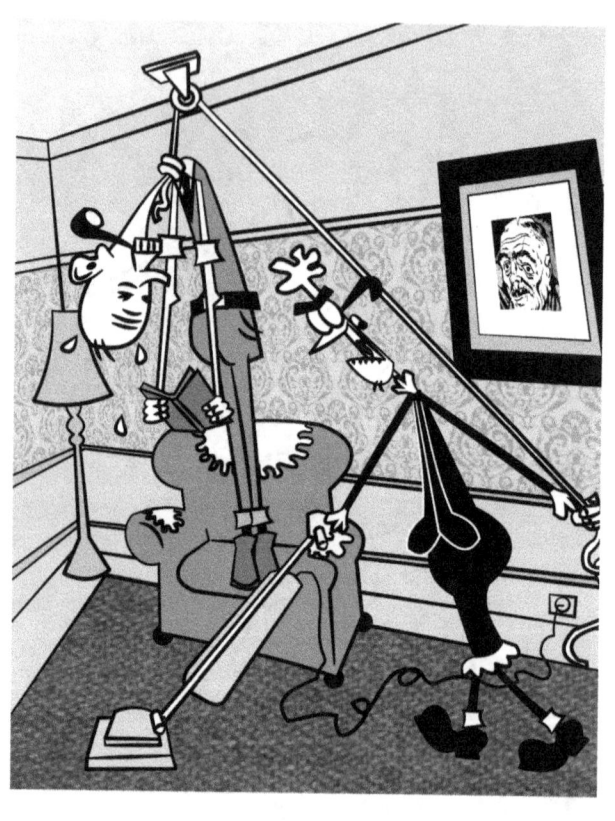

DIEDRE, ON OCCASIONS, WOULD HAVE TO RESORT TO IMPROVISITAION TO KEEP THE HOUSE PURE, UNSTAINED AND UNSULLIED.

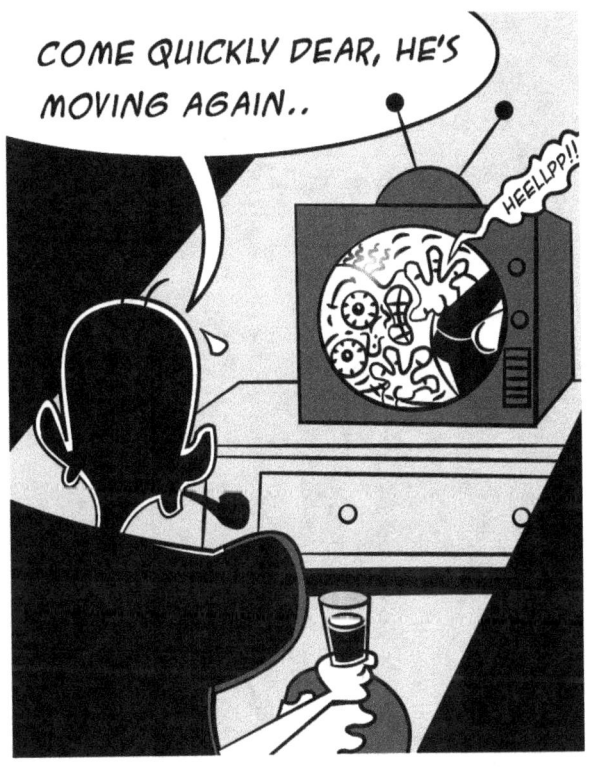

DIEDRE AND ALBERT TOOK GREAT DELIGHT
IN INVITING THE NEIGHBOURS OVER TO HELP
WITH THE EVENING'S ENTERTAINMENT.

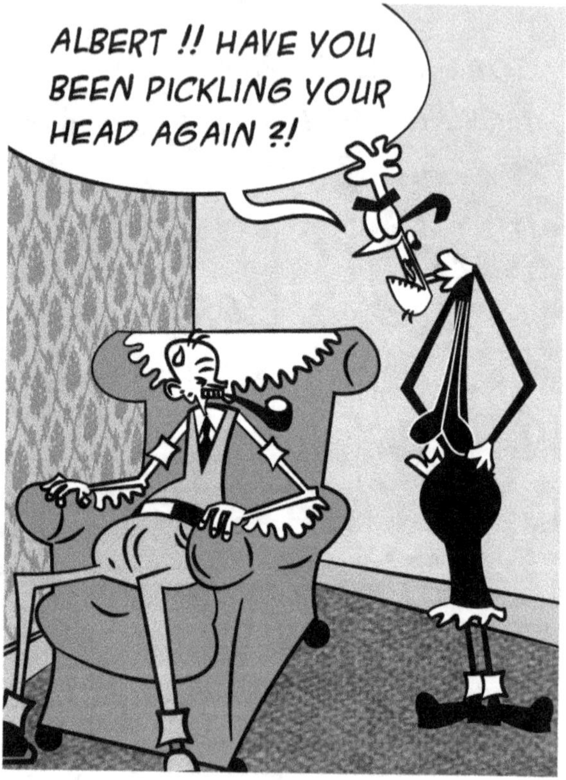
ALBERT !! HAVE YOU BEEN PICKLING YOUR HEAD AGAIN ?!

ON THE ODD OCCASIONS ALBERT CREPT INTO THE KITCHEN UNNOTICED, THE RESULTS COULD FREQUENTLY TURN OUT MESSY.

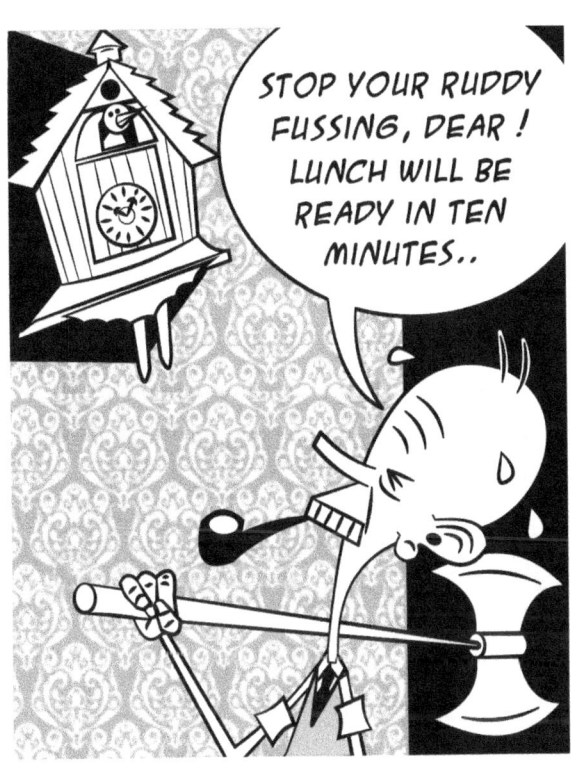

WHEN PHEASANT WASN'T AVAILABLE ON
THE MENU, ALBERT KNEW THAT WITH A
LITTLE PATIENCE, A DECENT ALERNATIVE
COULD READILY BE FOUND.

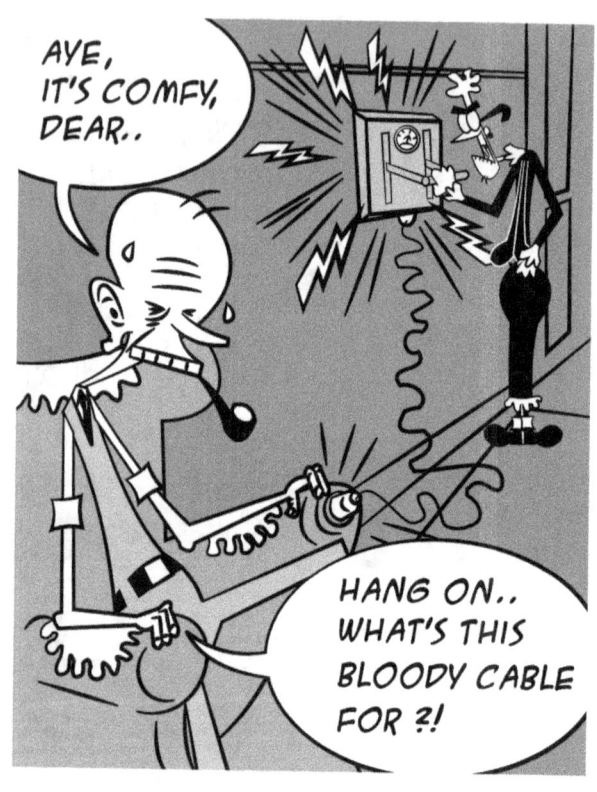

ALBERT'S COMFORT WAS OF GREAT IMPORTANCE TO DIEDRE. HIS INDOLENCE HOWEVER, WAS SOMETHING SHE CONSISTENTLY SOUGHT TO SABOTAGE.

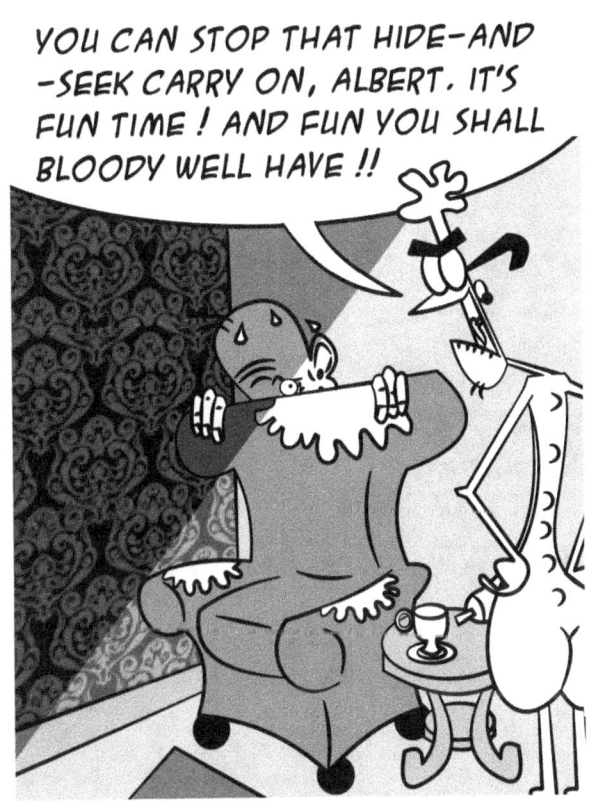

SATURDAY EVENINGS HELD A SPECIAL PLACE IN ALBERT'S TIMID YET RAPIDLY POUNDING HEART.

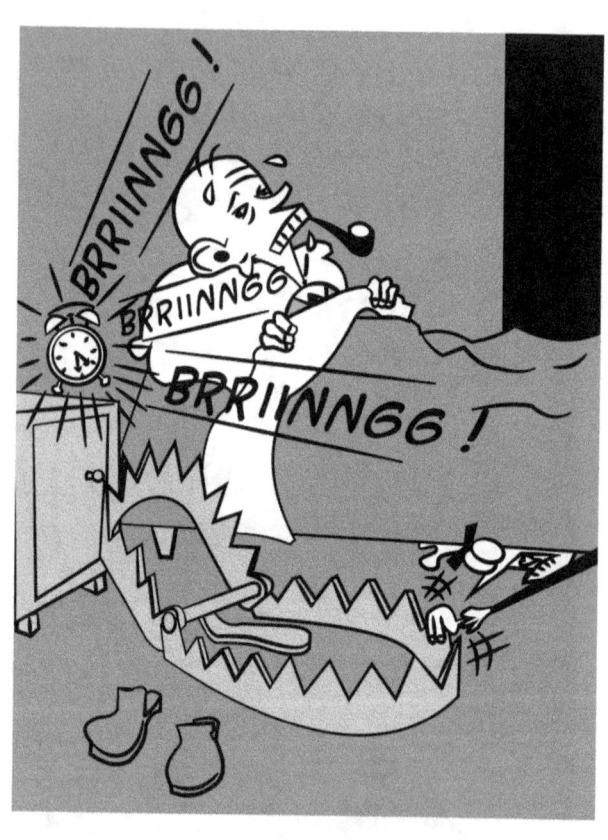

DIEDRE LIKED TO ENSURE ALBERT ENJOYED AN EARLY, REGULARLY RAMBUNCTIOUS START TO THE DAY.

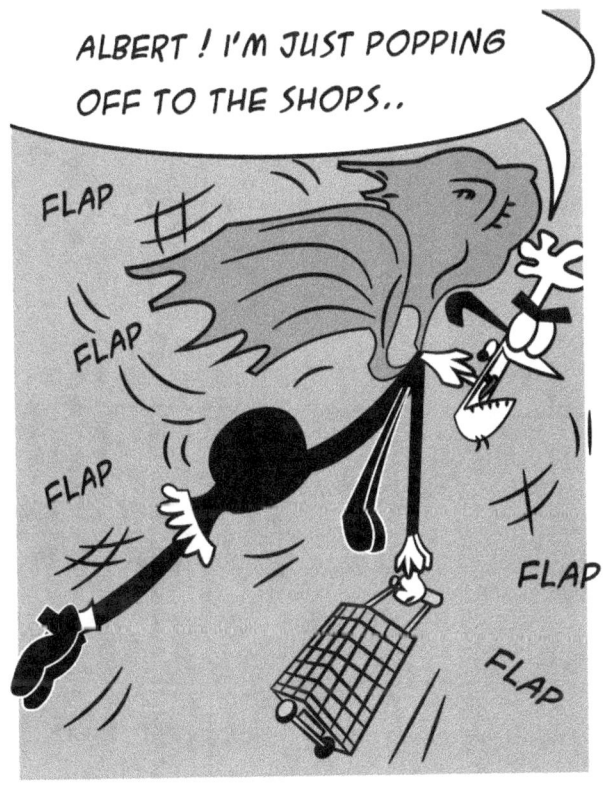

DIEDRES UNIQUE TALENTS ALLOWED HER TO GET TO THE SUPERMARKET QUICKLY AND WITH A MINIMUM OF FUSS.

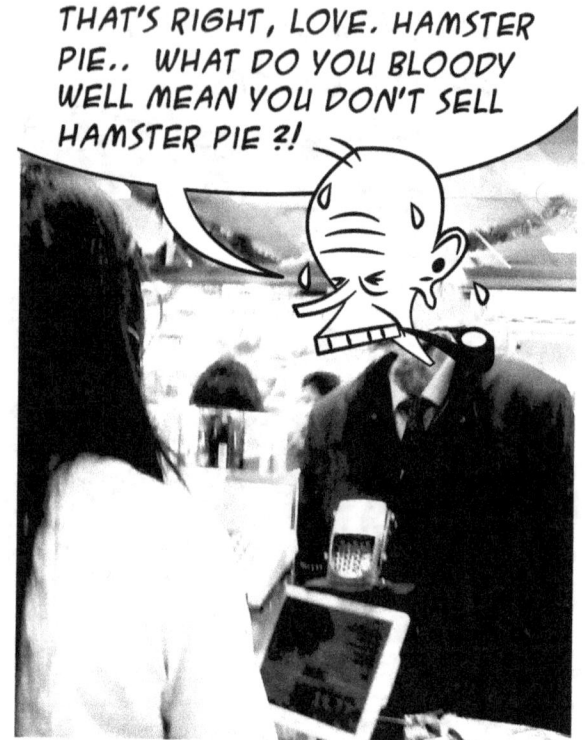

OF A WEEKEND, ALBERT COULD BE SEEN DUTIFULLY HEADING TO THE SUPERMARKET ON THE QUEST FOR QUALITY MEAT PRODUCE

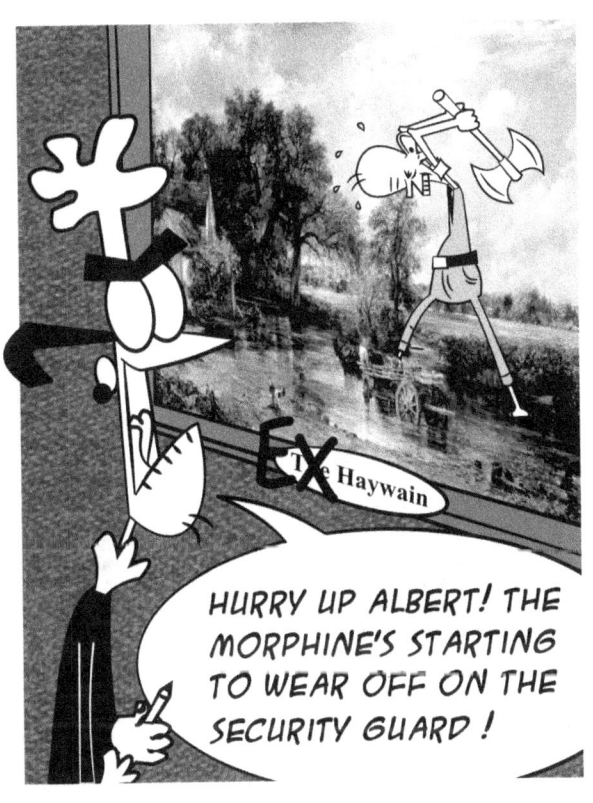

AS FINE ARTISTS THEMSELVES, DIEDRE AND ALBERT LIKED NOTHING BETTER THAN TO CREATE INTERACTIVE PERFORMANCE MASTERPIECES ON EXCURSIONS TO THE LOCAL ART GALLERY.

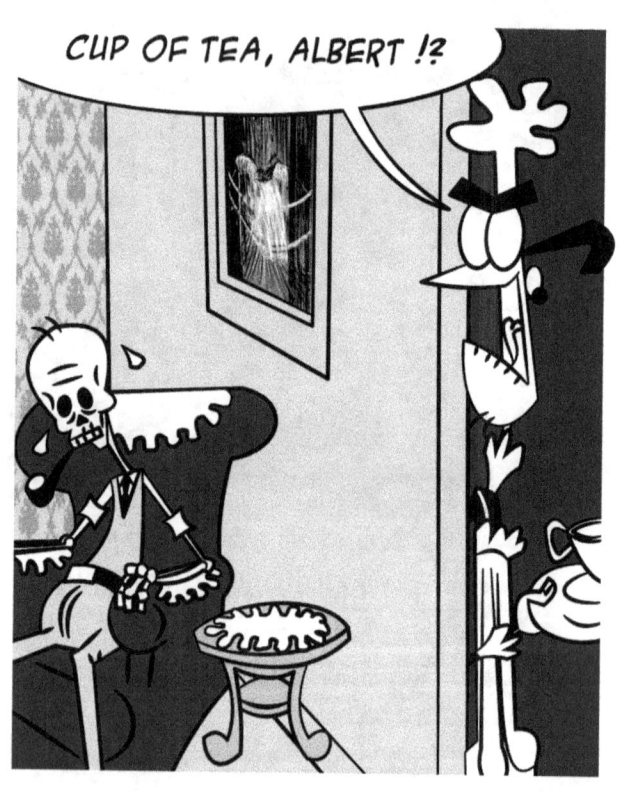

TEA OFTEN TOOK SOME TIME TO BREW
TO ALBERT'S PEDANTIC SPECIFICATION.

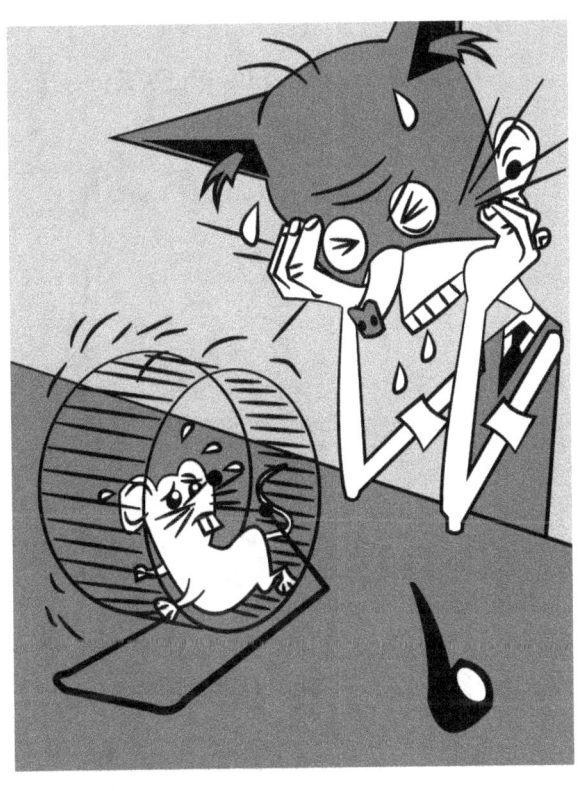

ALBERT PRIDED HIMSELF ON BEING
EFFERVESCENTLY ENTHUSIASTIC
WHEN ENSURING THAT THE HOUSE
PETS ENJOYED PLENTY OF EXERCISE.

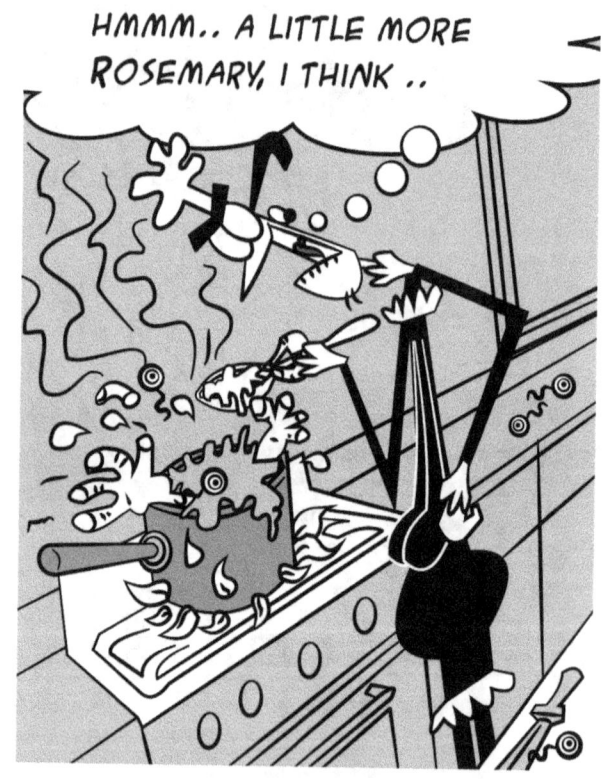

DIEDRE KNEW HER COOK BOOK TITLE "COOKING WITH NEIGHBOURS" WAS A GOOD ONE, BUT WAS RUNNING RAPIDLY OUT OF INGREDIENTS.

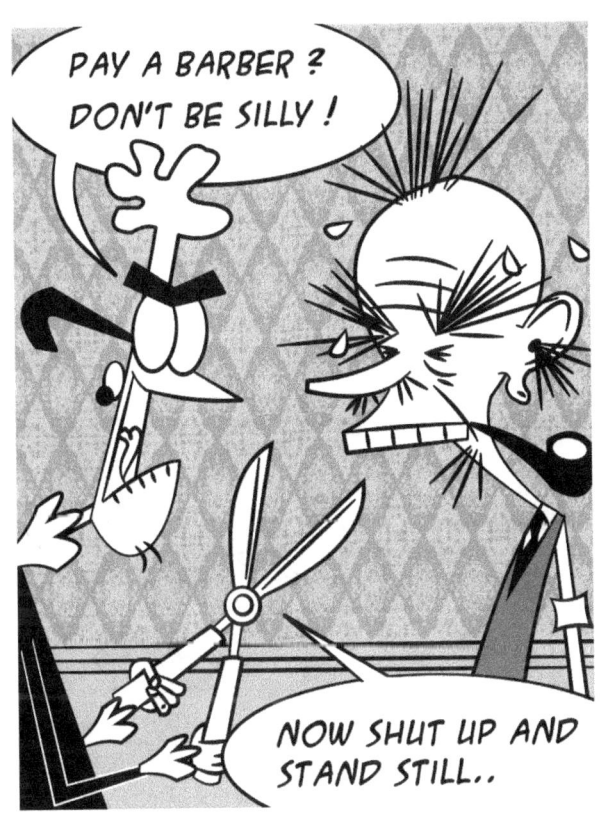

DIEDRE HABITUALLY KEPT A FIRM HAND
BOTH ON THE PURSE STRINGS AND ON HER
CONSPICUOSLY BLUNT HEDGE CLIPPERS.

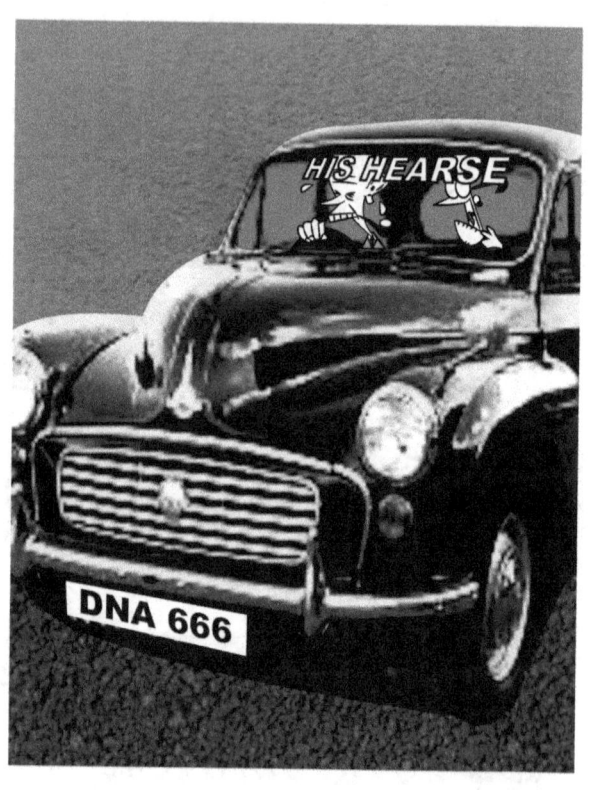

DIEDRE AND ALBERT SOMETIMES SAT
FOR HOURS IN THE MORRIS MINOR
PARKED IN THE GARAGE. DREAMING
OF ONE DAY KNOWING HOW TO
ACTUALLY START THE ENGINE

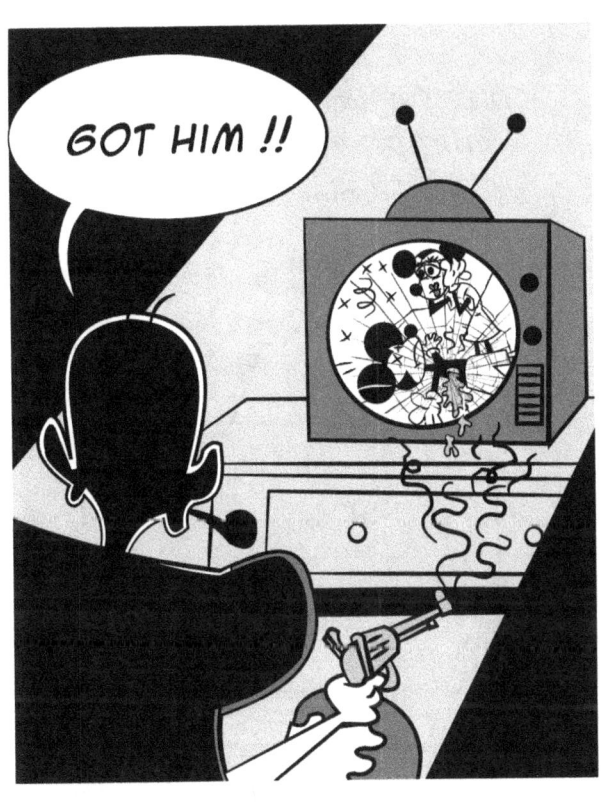

When the TV cartoons became a little boring, Albert relished adding a little zest by contributing his own storyline.

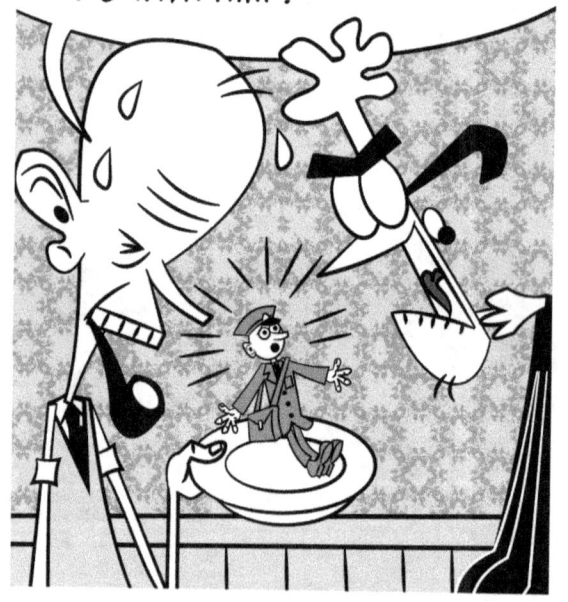

ALBERT'S CONSTANT DABBLING WITH
HIS HOME MADE SHRINKING MACHINE
SOMETIMES LEFT POST MAN PAT IN
AN AWKWARD PREDICAMENT.

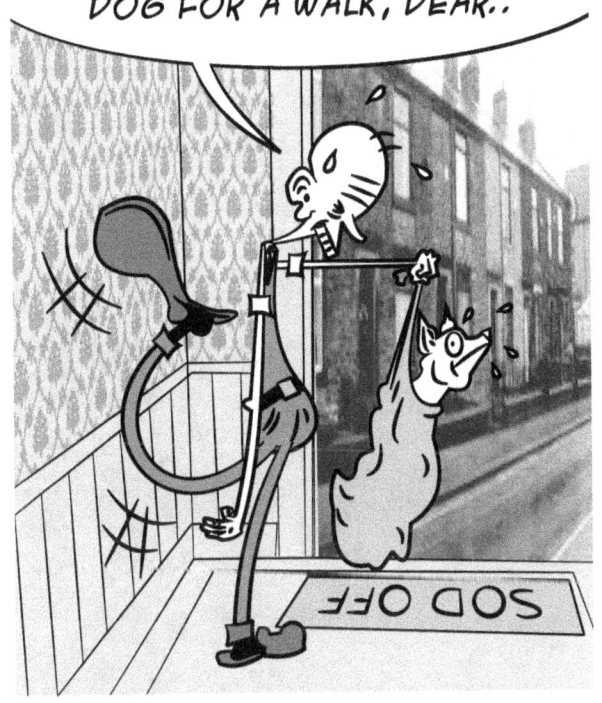

Helping the neighbours look after their pet's was a convenient way for Albert to keep himself held in a suitably low regard by the local community.

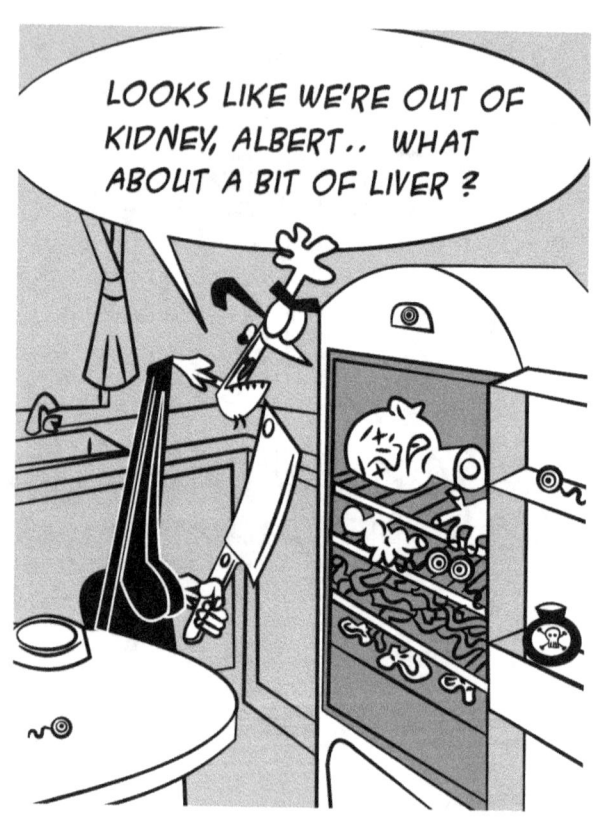

DIEDRE WAS FULLY AWARE THAT PROTEIN WAS AN INTEGRAL PART OF A HEALTHY BALANCED DIET.

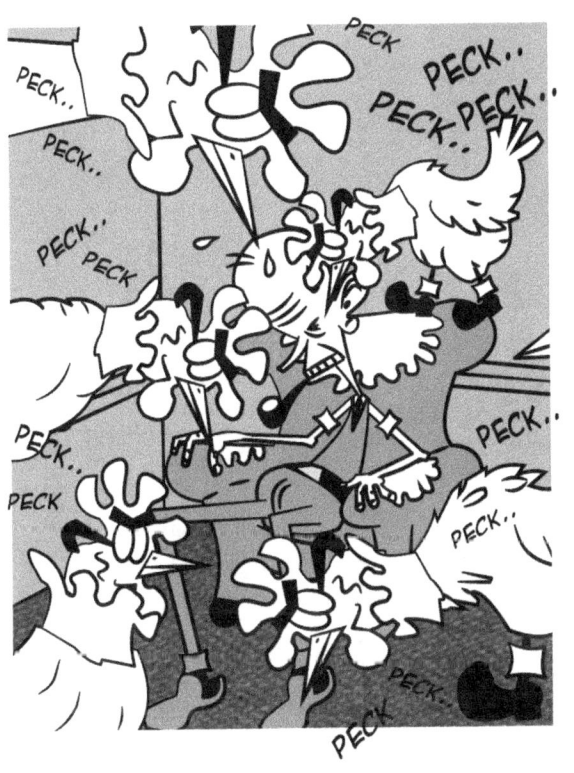

Albert often let the chickens come home to roost, but in general regretted using the cross cloning system he had invented to create them.

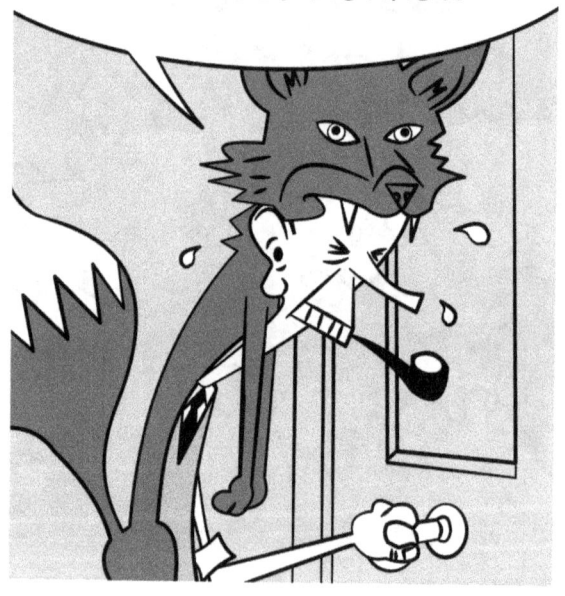

FORCING THE HENS TO GET A MOVE ON WITH THE EGG SUPPLY WAS A JOB ALBERT ADDRESSED WITH SOME ENTHUSIASTICALLY CREATIVE SOLUTIONS.

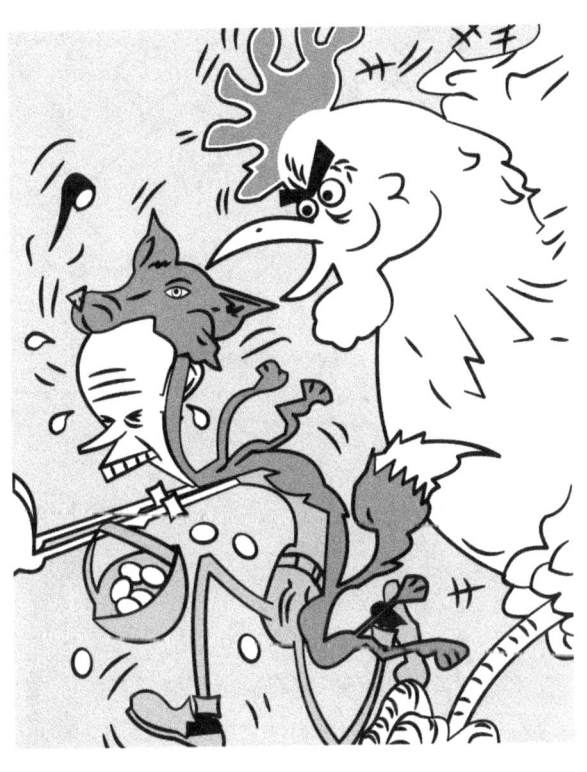

PREVENTING ALBERT'S ACQUISITION OF THE EGGS WAS SOMETHING THE CHICKENS TOOK TO WITH A MORE BASIC, BUT NO LESS ENTHUSIASTIC, SOLUTION OF THEIR OWN.

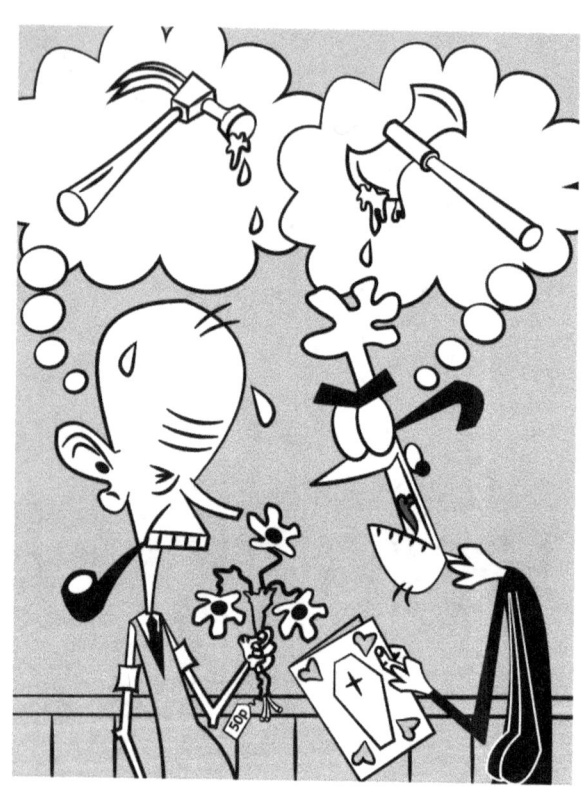

THE VALENTINE'S DAY MASSACRE.

THE PLANNING STAGE.

L'AMOUR TOUJOURS L'AMOUR.

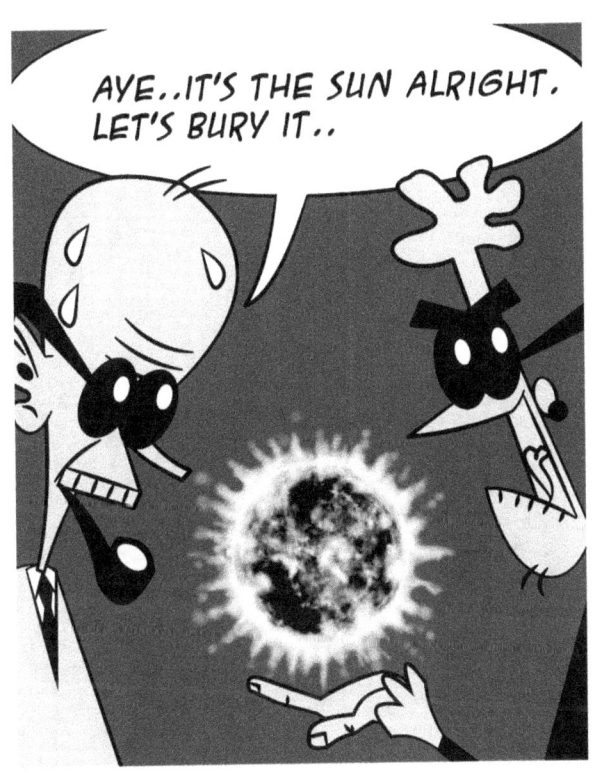

CAPTURING THE TRUE ESSENCE OF NATURE IN ALL OF IT'S HEAVENLY GLORY WAS CRUCIALLY IMPORTANT TO DIEDRE AND ALBERT...

THEN SMASHING IT UP.

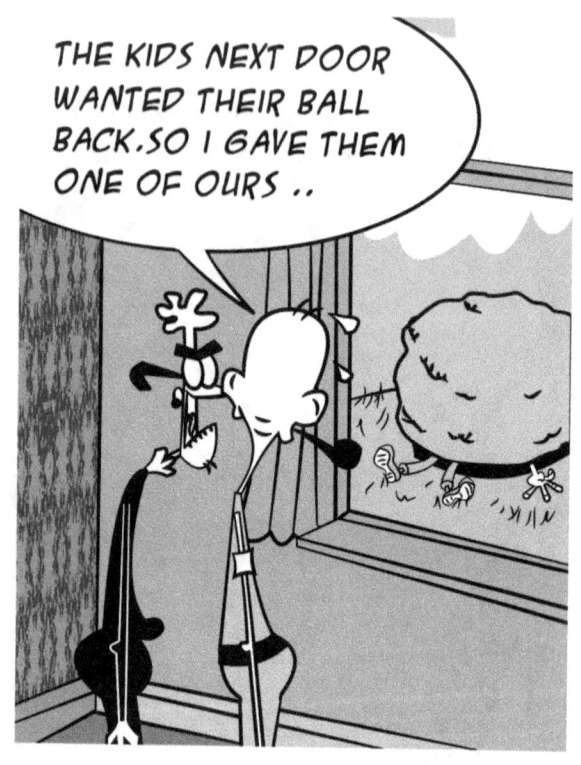

SELFLESSNESS WAS AN ESSENTIAL PART OF DIEDRE AND ALBERT'S HOLISTIC APPROACH TO THEIR UNREMITTING DESCENT INTO HELL.

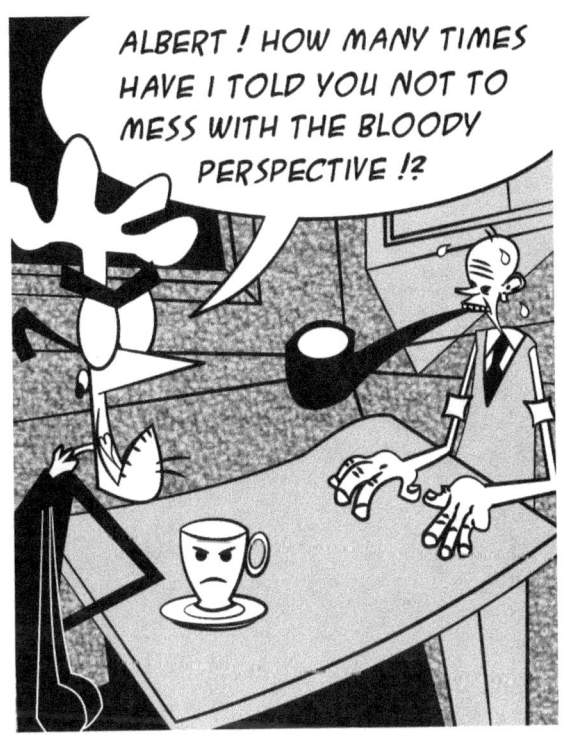

Albert's random but insistent meddling with the time space continuum sometimes made the kitchen walls turn a little furry and the breakfast Tea appear cold, sardonic and somewhat indifferent.

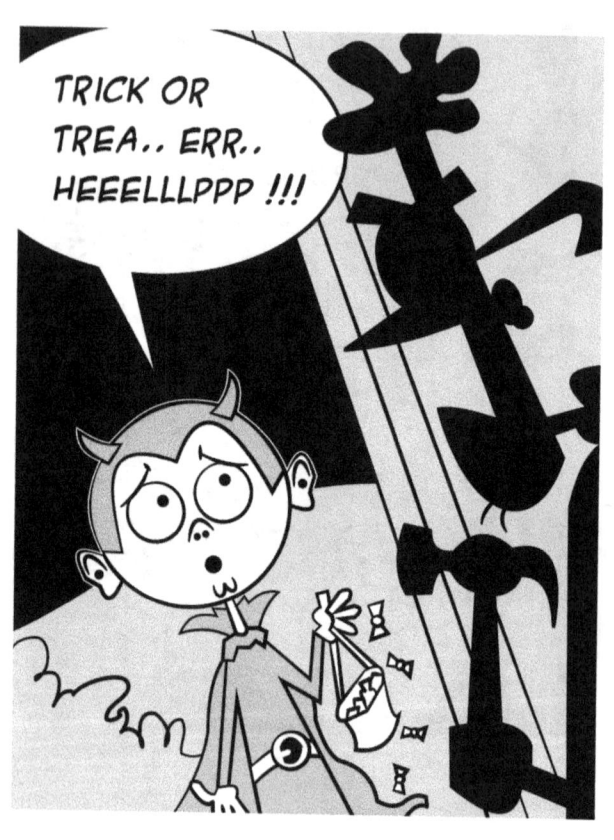

COME HALLOWEEN, DIEDRE GLEEFULLY ANTICIPATED THE VISIT OF THE LOCAL TRICK-OR-TREATERS.

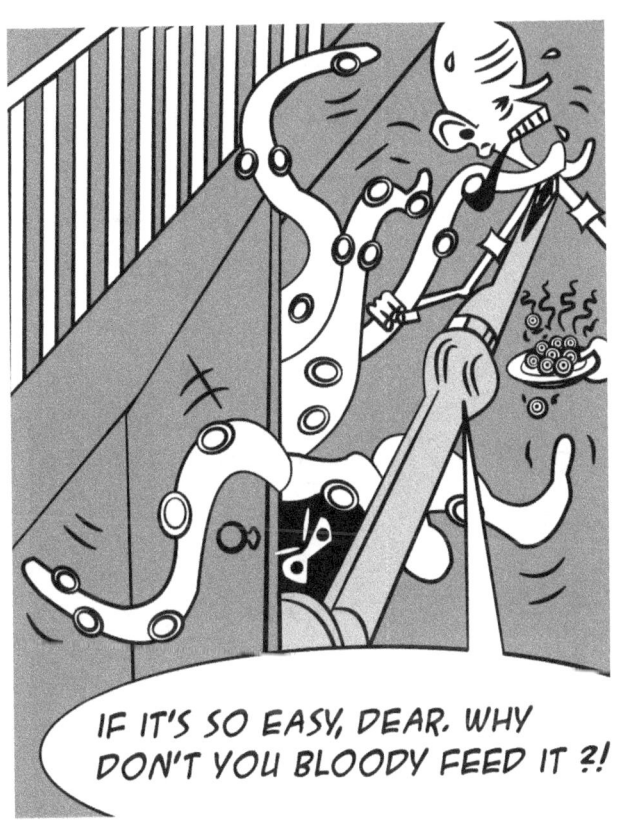

ALBERT HAD BEEN ASSIGNED THE SOLEMN
DUTY OF FEEDING THE PETS. IT WAS DIEDRE'S
SWORN DUTY TO MAKE SURE HE REGRETTED IT.

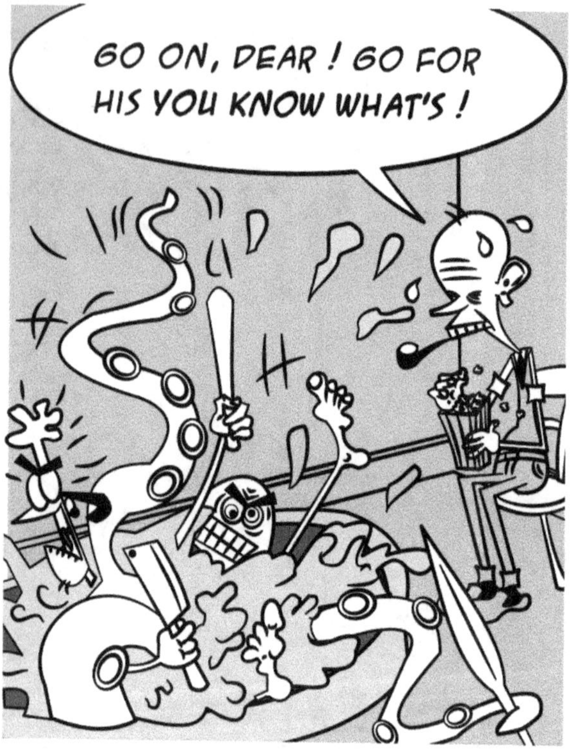
GO ON, DEAR ! GO FOR HIS YOU KNOW WHAT'S !

AFTER BINGO, FRIDAY NIGHT NAKED MUD WRESTLING WAS A REGULAR DATE IN THE DIEDRE AND ALBERT FUN-PACKED ENTERTAINMENT CALENDAR.

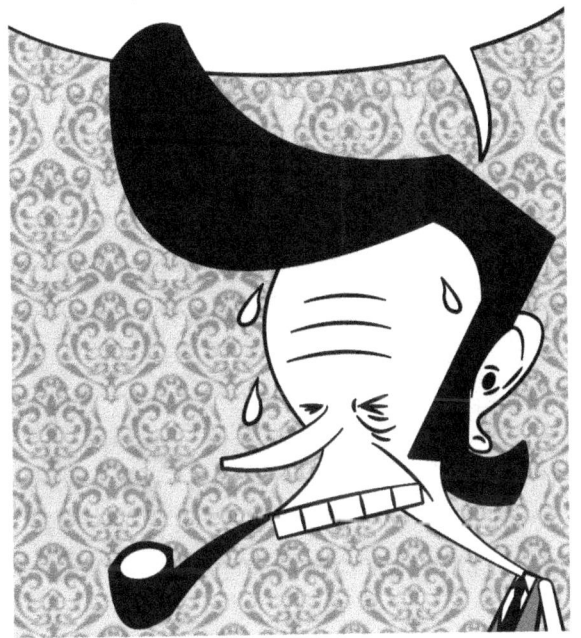

FOREVER THE DANDY, ALBERT LIKED
TO KEEP UP WITH THE CUTTING EDGE
FASHION ... OF 60 YEARS AGO.

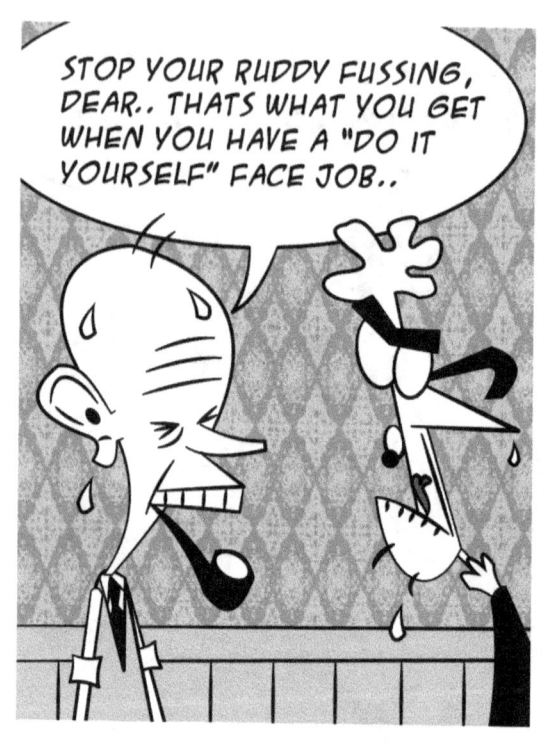

DIEDRE'S TIGHTNESS WITH THE PURSE
STRINGS MEANT SHE WOULD SOMETIMES
CUT HER NOSE OFF TO SPITE HER FACE.
THEN CAREFULLY STITCH IT BACK ONTO
THE OTHER SIDE OF HER HEAD.

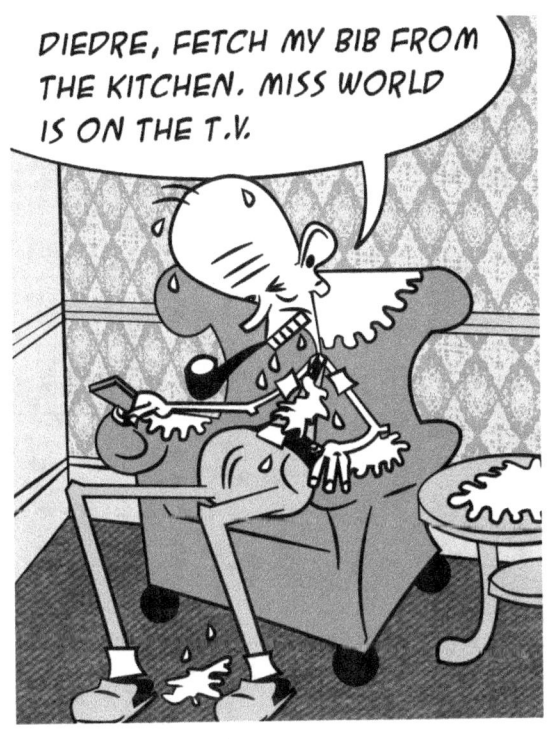

GOOD OLD FASHIONED BEAUTY CONTEST'S
WERE A GOOD OLD FASHIONED WAY FOR
ALBERT TO ENJOY DRIBBLING A STEADY
DROP OF GOOD OLD FASHIONED DROOL.

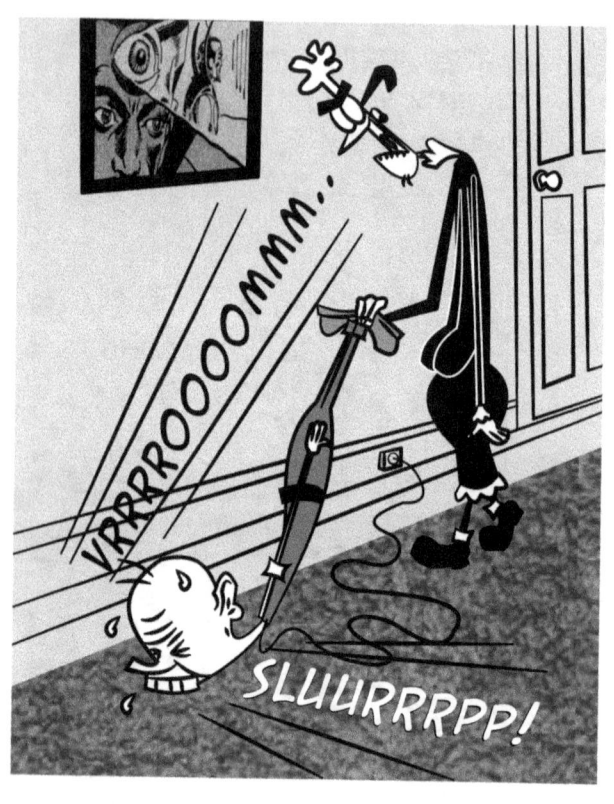

KEEPING THE SHAGPILE CLEAN WAS A CHORE THAT DIEDRE AND ALBERT TOOK SERIOUSLY.

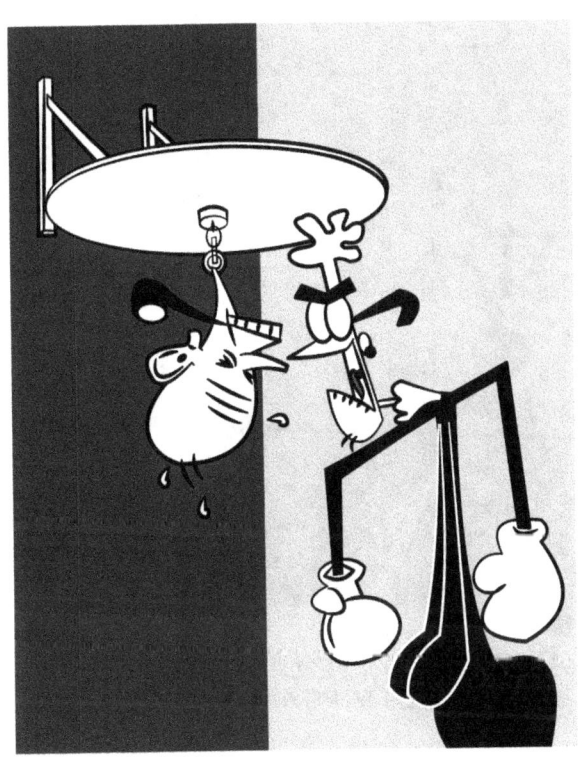

DIEDRE LIKED TO KEEP HERSELF IN GOOD PHYSICAL SHAPE. AS OFTEN AS NOT BY REWORKING ALBERT INTO A NOT SO GOOD PHYSICAL SHAPE.

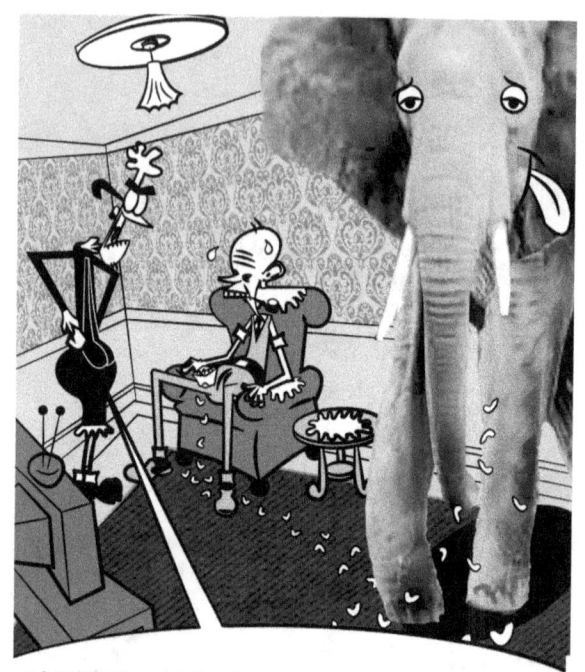

ALBERT.. YOU'VE LEFT A HOLE IN
YOUR BLOODY PEANUT BAG AGAIN.

EATING A FEW SNACKS WHILST WATCHING
TV WAS A SURE WAY FOR ALBERT TO LAND
HIMSELF IN ALL SORTS OF RIDICULOUS
PREDICAMENTS.

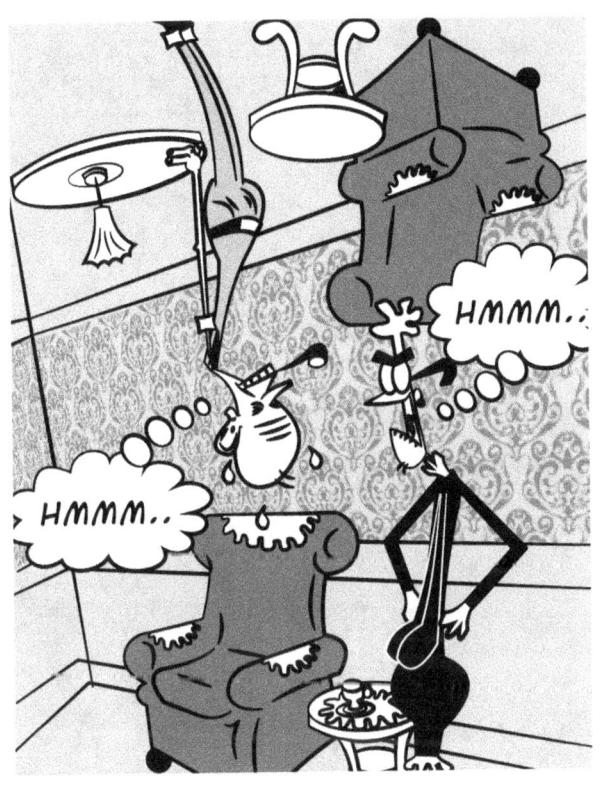

IT WAS NEVER A GOOD IDEA WHEN BOTH
DIEDRE AND ALBERT DECIDED TO MOVE
THE FURNITURE AT THE SAME TIME ...
WITHOUT CHECKING THE DIMENSIONS.

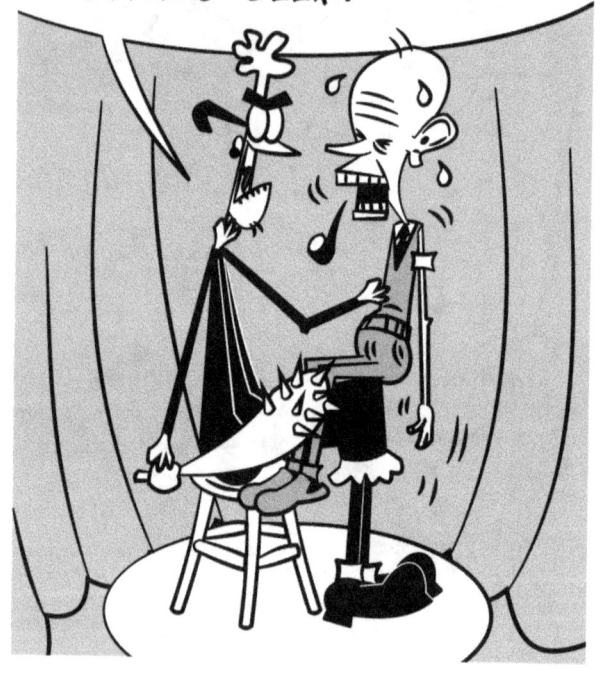

FOR DIEDRE AND ALBERT, ROLE PLAY WAS AN IMPORTANT WAY OF KEEPING ROMANCE ALIVE. EVEN IF IT MEANT ALBERT HAD TO SUFFER A FEW PLAYFUL CONTUSIONS.

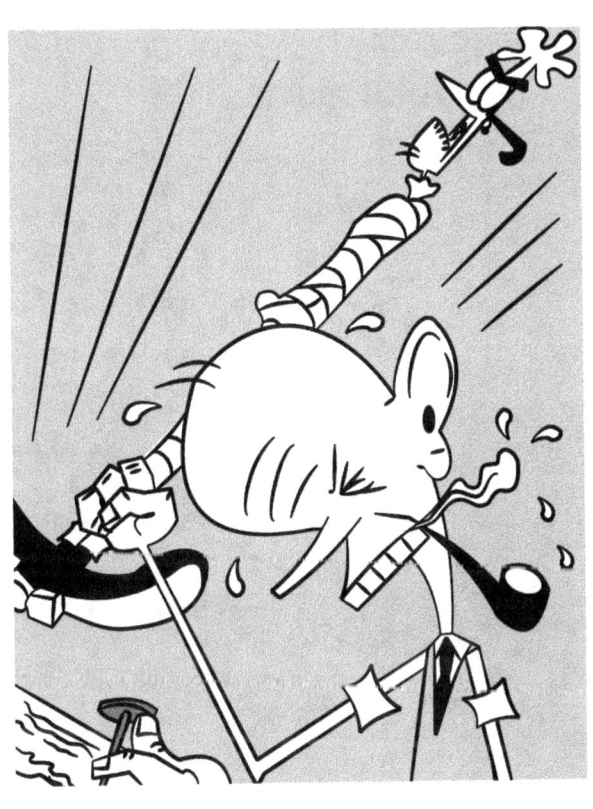

ALBERT KNEW PERFECTLY WELL THAT A BAD WORKMAN ALWAYS BLAMED HIS TOOLS, GIVING HIM GREAT COMFORT WHEN DOING A SPOT OF ABYSMAL DIY.

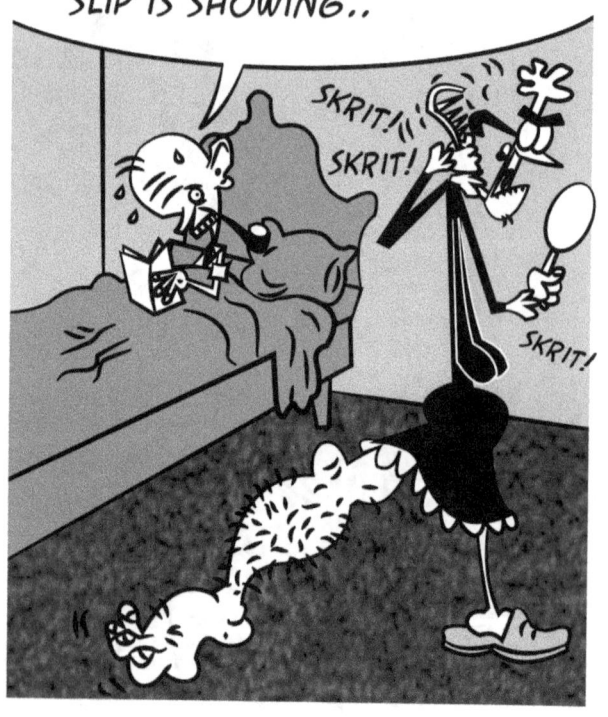

THE NERVOUS AGONY OF ANTICIPATION.

THE HEARTFELT PANG OF ROMANCE.

THE PSYCHOTIC PULSE OF FEAR.

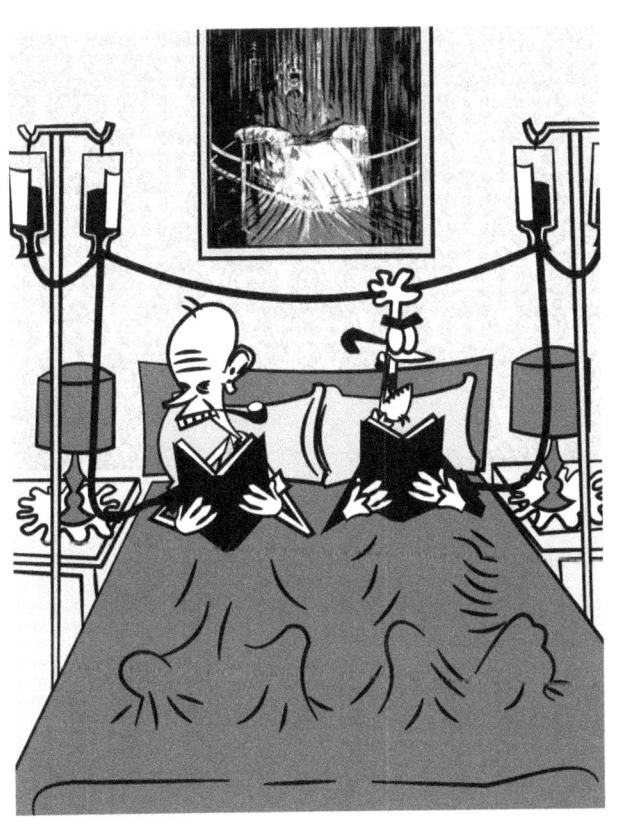

AND SO, TO BED..

A NOTE ABOUT THE AUTHOR:

ANDREW JOHNSON IS IN FACT, A.I. JOHNSON,
WITHOUT THE IAN BIT. BUT FOR SOME REASON
DECIDED TO MAKE THIS BOOK
USING THE OTHER NAME.

CRAZY TIMES INDEED

IF ONLY I KNEW AS TO THE WHY
OR EVEN THE WHEN.

BOTH OF THEM WERE BORN IN MANSFIELD, ENGLAND,
ARE 342 YEARS YOUNG AND WRITE AND DRAW
DIEDRE AND ALBERT IN THEIR SPARE TIME.

THEY NOW NEED A VERY LONG LIE DOWN.

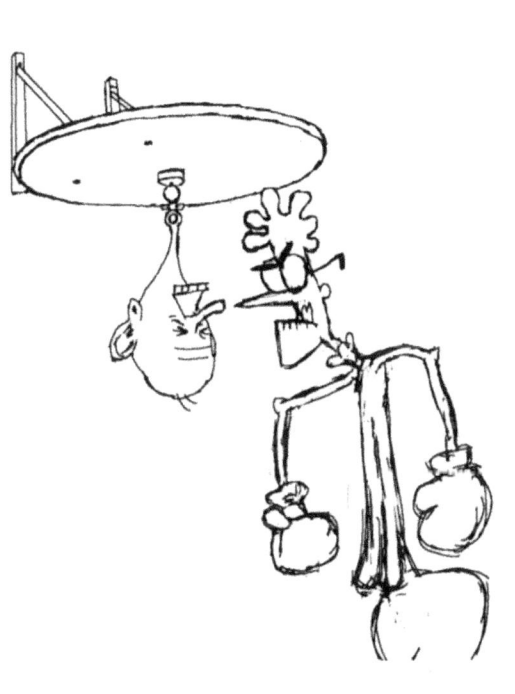

www.ingramcontent.com/pod-product-compliance
Lightning Source LLC
Chambersburg PA
CBHW070427240526
45472CB00020B/1511